PHILOSOPHERS OF THE SPIRIT

PASCAL

PHILOSOPHERS OF THE SPIRIT

PASCAL

Edited by
Robert Van de Weyer

Hodder & Stoughton
LONDON   SYDNEY   AUCKLAND

British Library Cataloguing in Publication Data:
A record for this book is available from the British Library.

ISBN 0 340 69403 3

Typeset in Monotype Columbus by
Strathmore Publishing Services, London N7.

Printed and bound in Great Britain by
Mackays of Chatham PLC, Chatham, Kent

Hodder and Stoughton Ltd,
A division of Hodder Headline PLC
338 Euston Road, London NW1 3BH

CONTENTS

SERIES INTRODUCTION

The first task of philosophers is to ask questions – the questions which lurk in all our minds, but which, out of fear or confusion, we fail to articulate. Thus philosophers disturb us. The second task of philosophers is to try and answer the questions they have asked. But since their answers are inevitably only partial, philosophers both interest and infuriate us. Their third and most important task is to stimulate and inspire us to ask questions and seek answers for ourselves.

The human psyche or spirit has always been the main – although not the only – focus of philosophy. And inevitably when the psyche is explored, the gap between religion and philosophy rapidly narrows. Indeed for philosophers in the more distant past there was no gap at all, since philosophy was an aspect of theology and even mysticism. Although religious institutions are now quite weak, questions of spiritual philosophy are being asked more keenly and urgently than ever.

This series is an invitation to readers, with no philosophical training whatever, to grapple with the great philosophers of the spirit. Most philosophy nowadays is served in the form of brief summaries, written by commentators. Each of these books contains an introduction to the life and ideas of the philosopher in question. But thereafter the reader encounters the philosopher's original words – translated into modern English. Usually the words are easy to follow; sometimes they are more difficult. They are never dull, always challenging, and frequently entertaining.

INTRODUCTION

Blaise Pascal faced with courageous honesty the central dilemma confronting the human spirit in seventeenth-century Europe, and which now confronts the human spirit across the entire globe: that human beings continue to have a very strong need and desire for religion; yet religious beliefs are unprovable, and for many people implausible. For Pascal this dilemma was very personal, and at times extremely painful. He was one of the most intelligent men of his day, who even in his late teens was making scientific discoveries; so he was acutely aware that the orthodox creeds of the Church defied scientific enquiry. Yet his family was deeply religious, and he yearned for the comfort and tranquillity that religion can bring.

His genius lay in his response to this dilemma. He saw that human experience at every level is caught up in paradox. There is the paradox of reason and emotion: that we are simultaneously guided by cold, rational logic, and by warm, passionate feelings. There is the paradox of weakness and strength: that in weakness we find our greatest source of strength.

There is the paradox of fame and obscurity: that many people, Pascal included, crave the respect and adulation of others; yet at best only a tiny minority can be satisfied, and even they remain obscure outside their own town or country. There is the economic paradox: that human beings have apparently unlimited material wants, but possess only limited resources to meet them. There is the paradox of lust: that a man can be overwhelmed with desire for a woman, believing that only with her he will be happy, and that he will destroy his family, his career, his reputation and everything else that brings happiness, in order to get her. There is the paradox of courage: that many people are prepared to die for their country or their opinions, when the deepest instinct in the human breast is for survival. And there is the paradox of belief and doubt: that human beings can simultaneously believe something fervently, and be sceptical about it.

While many of his scientific contemporaries shied away from paradox, preferring the intellect to move forwards in a straight line, Pascal's fluid mind revelled in it. And he saw the religious dilemma as the fundamental paradox on which all the others rest. To the chagrin of many theologians, Pascal recognised that religion is primarily a matter of the heart, not the head, so resolving the religious dilemma is bound up with resolving the paradox of reason and emotion.

Equally religion arises from weakness, while scientific enquiry is an assertion of strength; religion sanctifies poverty and obscurity, while scientific technology offers the means towards greater prosperity; religion grapples with our destructive lusts, seeking to redirect them, while reason makes plain their folly; religion can inspire courage, while reason tempers it.

But, while observing and analysing these other paradoxes, Pascal reserved his main attention for the paradox of faith and doubt. He envied earlier, pre-scientific ages when the causes for doubt were much less strong; but as a man of the highest intellectual calibre, living at the start of the modern age of science, he saw clearly that the pillars of religious belief were shaking – and in the years to come would be shaken with increasing ferocity. His resolution of the paradox is ingenious, and it has inspired and infuriated people in equal measure ever since. Since no one can be certain whether the tenets of religion are true or false, Pascal argued, individuals have no choice but to take a gamble. If they wager that religion is true, then they will pursue happiness through the practice of virtue and meditation; if they wager that religion is false, they will pursue happiness through the acquisition of material wealth and fame. Once religion is perceived in these terms, Pascal claimed, rational individuals will inevitably gamble on its truth – for two reasons. In the first place, even on this earth religious people tend to be more content and happy than those pursuing material gain; so even if their contentment is based on an illusion, it nonetheless is worth possessing. Secondly, the potential reward for gambling correctly on religion is eternal bliss, whereas the rejection of religion offers no reward at all.

By this argument Pascal was giving rational grounds for embracing religion, while acknowledging that the appeal of religion is to the heart. Nonetheless Pascal retained great respect for those who studied carefully the claims of religion, making every effort to understand them, and then on balance rejected them. In Pascal's eyes the real enemies were those who were indifferent to religion: who could not be bothered to study religion, and who simply drifted through life without aim or purpose. The attitude of such people was so foreign to Pascal's intense and ambitious temperament, that he regarded them as little less than monsters.

While an individual may accept religion on the basis of a calculated risk, Pascal knew from his own experience that the process of conversion is far deeper than this, involving a revolutionary change in the entire personality. And he described in detail the stages of this revolution. The first stage is joy at the discovery of God's love, followed quickly by confusion, as the soul finds herself still strongly attached to material pleasures. As the soul learns to break these attachments, she starts to despise every aspect of life that is not eternal, including even human relationships. This leads to a form of spiritual pride, in which the soul looks down on people who are still subject to earthly desires; and she feels angry at the vast number in this state. But gradually pride and anger give way to warmer emotions. The soul realises that many earthly desires are not in themselves sinful, and can be pursued quite legitimately. And this perception leads the soul to feel great love and compassion for all people, engendering a wish to serve them in practical ways. Soon love for others carries the soul upwards to the source of all love, God himself; and the soul sets off on a mystical journey, which eventually takes her into God's presence.

During the final years of his short life, Pascal undoubtedly made rapid progress along the mystical path. And it is his combination of mysticism and rationality which gives him special importance today. If the tenets of orthodox belief were hard to accept three and a half centuries ago, they are far harder now. Yet at some level, and at some periods of their lives, most people are still drawn towards religion. Many become willing to take the wager which religion offers; and the prospect of embarking on a mystical journey, in which the soul will find peace and serenity, is the main incentive.

* * *

Blaise Pascal was born in 1623 at Clermont (now Clermont-Ferrand) in Auvergne. His father, Etienne, was a successful lawyer with a keen interest in science. He had an older sister, Gilberte, and a younger sister, Jacqueline, both of whom in adulthood were to influence deeply his religious outlook. In 1626 their mother died, and five years later Etienne settled with his three children in Paris. He directed Blaise's education himself, demanding from his son the highest intellectual performance. Blaise responded; and at the age of twelve he is said to have discovered for himself the first thirty-two propositions of Euclid's geometry, as well as Pythagoras' theorem. Etienne Pascal's interest in science brought him into contact with the leading intellectual figures of the day, including Descartes, whom he invited to his house. Blaise was allowed to converse with them, and this stimulated his mind further. At the age of sixteen Blaise published a paper on the geometry of cones which caused a great stir among mathematicians, arousing Descartes' envy.

In 1638 Etienne Pascal joined a protest against the financial policy of Cardinal Richelieu, the effective ruler of France. The cardinal turned his forces against the protesters, and Etienne was forced to flee with his family back to Auvergne. Happily the cardinal was extremely fond of Jacqueline, who was now exceptionally pretty, and in 1640 he partially relented. He appointed Etienne Pascal to be in charge of the collection of taxes in Rouen. Within two years Blaise had invented the first calculating machine to assist his father; and a number were manufactured by Rouen craftsmen and installed in the tax office. Blaise then turned his attention to the problems of vacuums, eventually writing papers which secured his place among the first rank of scientists.

In 1646 Etienne Pascal badly injured his leg; and he was treated by two brothers who devoted their spare time to setting broken bones, making no charge for their services. They were members of a religious group, known as Jansenists after their founder, which was renowned for its strict moral and spiritual standards. This encounter with Jansenism transformed the entire family. Etienne, now an old man, immediately adopted the Jansenist way of life, devoting his final years to prayer and acts of charity. Jacqueline, whose interests until now had been poetry, drama and fine clothes, decided that she wished to become a nun at Port Royal, a convent supervised by a Jansenist priest. Gilberte, who had married, became an ardent supporter of Port Royal. Blaise was more cautious, and initially merely acknowledged religion as a valid object of enquiry. But the enthusiasm of his sisters, on whom he was emotionally dependent, gradually eroded his resistance.

In 1651 Etienne died. Jacqueline, who had delayed her religious vocation in order to nurse her father, went at once to Port Royal. For the first time in his life, Blaise found himself alone. An interior battle now began. As he reflected on his life until then, he felt deep resentment against the intellectual, and more recently spiritual, demands which his father had imposed. He resented too the emotional dominance of his sisters, especially Jacqueline; and by way of revenge he entered a long and acrimonious wrangle with Port Royal over the 'dowry' that Jacqueline should give to the convent. Reacting against his family, he tried to adopt a dissolute life, joining the social activities of other wealthy young men. But he still felt compelled to continue his scientific researches; and religious questions never ceased to disturb him.

Quite suddenly, on the night of 23 November 1654, he had an experience in which he felt the love and joy of God deep within him. He recorded the experience on a fragment of paper which he kept for the rest of his life sewn into the lining of his jacket. In this record, which he entitled *The Memorial*, he accuses himself of having denied and crucified Christ, because his own pride prevented him from embracing the gospel of Christ. Yet he recognises that the only path to true and lasting happiness is the total renunciation of all earthly ambition, and thence total submission to Christ as his master.

Two months later he went to stay at Port Royal, putting himself under the direction of one of the chaplains. Pascal embarked on an intensive course of spiritual and theological reading, applying himself to religion with the same intellectual intensity that he had applied to science. This soon led him back to science, because he felt impelled by God to use his technological skills in the service of the poor. In the spring of 1655 he went to a large marshland in Poitou, where he designed a complex system of drains to provide fertile fields; these were then offered to landless peasants.

In January 1656 Pascal returned to Port Royal for a second retreat. But by now the Jansenists were being accused by the ecclesiastical authorities of heresy. The theological issues were abstruse; but, as Pascal saw clearly, the real objection to the Jansenists was that their spiritual devotion and charitable activities were a living censure of the corrupt laxity of most bishops and priests. Pascal responded by writing a series of *Provincial Letters* in defence of the Jansenists. They were an immediate success, rallying public support to the Jansenists' side. He demolished the opponents of the Jansenists with a mixture of logic and derision, expressing his view in taut, concise prose which contrasted sharply with the pompous circumlocutions of most theological writings. His main target was not corruption as such, but hypocrisy: the gap between the high ideals which bishops and priests preach, and their actual way of life. He thus called all Christians to try and close that gap, living up to the standards which they profess.

Amidst this controversy Pascal continued to find time for his scientific work; and in 1657 he organised an international competition to solve the puzzle of the cycloid – the path traced by a ball on a roulette wheel. None of the entries satisfied him, and eventually he solved the puzzle himself. But religious questions were now uppermost in his mind, and he began to plan an *Apology for the Christian Religion*. His intention was to demonstrate to sceptics that Christianity was quite plausible; and that, although its tenets would always be open to doubt, the rational individual should on balance accept them and live as if they were true. By 1658 he had drawn up a plan for this work, and was beginning to write parts of the text. The first part would analyse the various paradoxes of the human condition, which not even the most brilliant minds can resolve by rational means. The second part would explore the psychology of those who are indifferent to religion, showing the wretchedness of their condition. And the third part would show how religious commitment resolves the paradoxes and brings interior happiness.

Pascal had never enjoyed robust health; as a child he had frequently been sick, and as an adult he claimed that he never passed a day without physical suffering. At the beginning of 1659 his condition began to deteriorate, so that he could only work for brief periods. He was probably suffering from some form of cancer, and in 1660 he enjoyed a period of remission, enabling him to write further pieces for the *Apology*. But in 1661 his sister Jacqueline died at Port Royal; and the reason given for her premature death was her distress at the relentless persecution which the convent was enduring at the hands of the ecclesiastical authorities. This persecution reached a climax the following year when an edict was issued, condemning one of the chaplains at Port Royal as a heretic. The members of the convent were required to sign an unconditional acceptance of the edict, or else face excommunication; after much anguished debate they signed. Pascal was devastated by his sister's death, and appalled by Port Royal's capitulation. By the start of 1662 his health was again worsening.

The spring of 1662 saw the fulfilment of his final practical project. Soon after his conversion he had conceived the idea of running a bus service across Paris, with the profits going for the relief of the poor. He had encountered various difficulties, but in March the first bus began to run, with tickets at five sous. By June, however, he was so ill that his sister Gilberte, living in the heart of the Latin Quarter of Paris, took him in, and nursed him for the last weeks of his life.

He died in great pain, but apparently at spiritual peace, on 19 August 1662, at the age of thirty-nine.

* * *

At the time of his death, Pascal's reputation was vast. Leading mathematicians and scientists throughout western Europe, including Christopher Wren, hailed him as an intellectual genius. And connoisseurs of the arts recognised the *Provincial Letters* as one of the supreme literary achievements of the century, pioneering a new style of prose. But of the book which Pascal had spent the last four years of his life planning, only his intimate friends were aware. To them Pascal was a man of great sanctity, who through great interior struggle had attained a profound understanding of divine truth, and who had learnt to bend both his intense emotions and his magisterial intellect to God's will. These friends now set about the task of putting together the fragments of text into a form which could be published.

Pascal's method was to write his thoughts on large sheets of paper, putting a horizontal line under each entry. Once a sheet was filled, he cut it into strips along the horizontal lines, so each strip corresponded to one entry. He divided the strips into twenty-eight groups, according to his proposed chapter headings. Finally he put a hole in the corner of each strip, and threaded string through the strips of each group, creating bundles. Unfortunately at the time of his death he had cut and classified only about a third of the large sheets, leaving two-thirds unclassified; thus his friends could only guess into which chapter these should go. Despite these difficulties they managed to bring out the first edition in 1670 under the title *Pensées* – a title which has stuck. The following century all the uncut sheets were chopped up; and together with the existing strips, they were pasted into a large album. Unfortunately the order of entry was largely dictated by the dimensions of the album, so fragments of the correct size were chosen to fill each page. As a result it has become even harder to discern Pascal's intended scheme.

Yet for the reader who is turning to Pascal for inspiration, this randomness is to some degree an advantage. Pascal was not a systematic thinker, as his method of composition demonstrates. He had flashes of insight, which can simultaneously dazzle the reader with their intellectual brilliance, and inspire the reader with their spiritual intensity. To read the *Pensées* is thus like looking at the stars in the night sky: occasionally patterns can be discerned, but each source of light can be appreciated by itself. Readers are left free to integrate Pascal's insights into their outlook in their own way.

Today inevitably Pascal's scientific work is largely forgotten, except by specialist historians: scientists are rightly so focused on the future that they pay little attention to their antecedents. The *Provincial Letters* are still enjoyed as masterpieces of prose and polemic. But it is his *Pensées* on which Pascal's continuing reputation largely depends. The first edition, less than a decade after his death, made surprisingly little impression; but with each passing century, as the reasons for doubting religion grow stronger, his thoughts on religion grow more relevant. He speaks to the sceptical reader in a sceptical age, who recognises that the tenets of religion can never be known for certain, and yet who deeply desires to be religious; he offers a means of combining intellectual honesty with genuine faith. But it is a measure of his genius that he also speaks to evangelicals who, from John Wesley onwards, have warmed to his profound analysis of the process of conversion; for them Pascal is a pioneer in the psychology of religion. And for all his profundity Pascal is a pleasure to read, his fast, fluid mind making even the dullest philosophical topic seem exciting.

Modern scholars have continued the task – which is ultimately vain – of trying to reproduce Pascal's original plan for the *Pensées*. In this present edition his thoughts are categorised under two broad headings. The first, entitled 'Paradoxes', contains pieces which focus on the human dilemma in its many aspects. The second, entitled 'Resolutions', contains pieces on the meaning and purpose of religion. These form the first two chapters of this book; and the numbers after each section relate to the numbering scheme which has been used by scholars for the past century. These chapters are followed by two large sections from the *Pensées* which stand on their own: his comparison of religious faith with a wager; and his diatribe against those who have no interest in religion. The fifth chapter is the short piece he wrote on the night of his conversion in 1654; and the sixth chapter the longer reflection he wrote some months later on the stages of conversion. The final chapter was probably written in the last months of his life, in which he asks God to make good use of his sickness.

ROBERT VAN DE WEYER

I
PARADOXES

For some people fame is so sweet that they would do anything to achieve it – even die.

– 37

Human beings are naturally foolish and ignorant; only divine grace can make them wise, and enable them to perceive the truth. The two faculties which should help people to be wise and perceptive, the senses and reason, are engaged in a constant battle, in which one tries to deceive the other. The senses trick reason by showing only the outward appearance of things, rather than their inner reality. And this deception is worsened when the emotions disturb the senses.

– 45

'This is my dog,' says a child. 'This is my place in the sun,' says another child. There is the origin of human conflict.

– 64

Knowledge of physical science offers no consolation when we are morally confused. But knowledge of morality is always a consolation when we feel confused about the physical world around us.

– 67

If you do not drink any wine, you will never find the truth. If you drink too much wine, you will also never find the truth.

– 71

Considering that human beings are a combination of mind and matter, we should understand the relationship between the two. But we barely understand it at all. We cannot properly conceive what the body is; and the mind is even more mysterious to us. As to how mind and matters are connected, we are utterly baffled. In short, we are beyond our grasp.

– 72

People rarely take pleasure in hurting others. But in their foolish ignorance many people cannot find a way of satisfying their own desires without harming others.

– 74

Why is it that a person who is physically lame does not annoy us, while a lame mind does? It is because a person who is physically lame knows that we are walking straight, while the lame mind thinks our minds are lame. But we should feel sorry for the lame mind, not angry.

– 80

What we call natural principles are in the main habitual principles, learnt mainly from our parents. A change of habit will produce different principles, as experience shows. But there are some principles that are truly natural, and which habit cannot change. Equally there are some habitual principles that are unnatural.

– 92

Our aims and goals often change, because we realise that present pleasures are false, and thus should not be pursued. And our aims and goals are often confused, because it occurs to us that other pleasures are possibly equally false.

– 110

The soul is not simple, and it can never apply itself to a subject with simplicity. That is why the same thing can make us both laugh and cry.

– 112

Human beings can believe something and doubt it at the same time. Equally they can be simultaneously timid and bold.   – 125

The typical condition of the human being is uncertainty, boredom and anxiety.

                                                                                 – 127

How easily we develop new attachments which take us away from present comforts. A man will destroy his happy home for the sake of an attractive woman. Another will destroy his material security for the excitement of a few days' gambling. These things happen all the time.

                                                                                 – 128

When people complain of the hard work they must do, try giving them no work to do.

                                                                                 – 130

Human beings find nothing so intolerable as to be in a state of complete rest, without feelings, without activities, without interests, expending no effort. In that condition they feel aimless, lonely, inadequate, dependent, helpless and empty. And from the depths of their souls wells up a sense of boredom, gloom, depression, irritation, resentment and despair.

                                                                                 – 131

Small things can console us, because small things can upset us.

– 136

Human beings are obviously made for thinking. Therein lies their dignity and their special gift. Their whole duty is to think as they should. The proper order of thought is to begin with ourselves, and work outwards towards our creator, who also represents the purpose of our lives. So what do most people think about? Rarely about their creator. They think about dancing, playing the lute, singing, writing verse, gambling, waging war, becoming king. They never think what it means to be a king, or even an ordinary human being.

– 146

We do not care about our reputation in towns which we are merely passing through. But when we have to remain some time in a town, we do care about our reputation. How long must we stay in a town in order to care about our reputation? The greater is our vanity, and the higher is the value we put on ourselves, the shorter is this time.

– 149

Vanity is so firmly anchored in the human heart that a soldier, a labourer, a cook or a porter will expect to be admired. Even philosophers want admirers. Those who write essays and books criticising others want prestige from having written well; and those who read what they have written want prestige from being well-informed. Perhaps I who write this am motivated by the desire for admiration; and perhaps you, my readers …

— 150

Curiosity is a form of vanity. We usually only want to know something so that we can talk about it. We would never travel by sea to other countries, if we did not anticipate later describing them to our friends.

— 152

There are warlike people who would find no purpose or pleasure in life if they could not bear arms and fight battles; they would prefer death to peace. There are peace-loving people who dislike war so much that they would prefer to die rather than fight. There are many people who hold their particular opinions so dearly that they would rather die than give them up. This is all very remarkable, since it seems natural that people should prefer life above all things.

— 156

You would think that the vanity of worldly ambition and success would be obvious. Yet people are surprised and indignant to be told that seeking greatness is foolish. That is truly remarkable.

– 161

Consider the causes and effects of erotic love. The causes we do not understand. The effects can be terrifying. This indefinable feeling, which we often dismiss as trivial, can upset the entire world, inducing armies to wage war. If Cleopatra's nose had been shorter, the course of human history would have been different.

– 162

There are people who fill their lives with noise, entertainment and plans for the future. But if the noise and entertainment were taken away, they would be utterly bored. They would feel the emptiness of their lives without knowing its cause. And their plans for the future would seem futile.

– 164

Some people, when they realise the wretchedness and misery of human existence, devote the rest of their lives trying to divert their attention with idle amusements.

– 167

Despite death, illness and ignorance, human beings want to be happy; indeed, happiness is all they want, and they cannot help wanting it. But how should they go about attaining happiness? The best way would be to make themselves immortal. But since this is impossible, they just try to stop thinking about death, illness and ignorance.

– 168

When we are miserable, we seek consolation in idle amusements. Yet these amusements only make our condition worse, because they prevent us thinking about ourselves and discerning the cause of our misery. It is better that boredom be added to our misery, since boredom would drive us to look for a genuine means of escape.

– 171

We rarely keep our minds on the present. We nostalgically recall the past, regretting how quickly time has flown. We eagerly anticipate the future, finding it too slow in coming and wanting time to hurry. How foolish we are to dwell on times that do not belong to us, and ignore the only time that does. How vain we are to dream of times that do not exist, and to run away from the time that is real. The reason for our folly and vanity is that the present is often painful. We push it out of sight because it distresses us.... The result is that we never actually live, but hope to live. And since we are constantly planning how to be happy, we never really are happy.

— 172

We know so little about ourselves that many people think they are going to die, when in fact they are quite well; and many people think they are quite well, when in fact they are at the point of death.

— 175

Anyone who can rejoice when things go well, without becoming sad or angry when things go wrong, has found the secret of happiness.

— 181

When I consider the briefness of my span of life, compared with the eternity that comes before and after; when I consider the smallness of the space I occupy, compared with the infinity of space of which I know nothing, and which knows nothing of me – then I am amazed and awe-struck to see myself now and here, rather than in some other time and place. There is no reason for me to be here rather than elsewhere, to live now rather than sometime else. Who put me here? By whose command and act were this time and space allotted to me?

– 205

You may become famous within your own town or country; but to most people in the world, your name means nothing.

– 207

If we were alone in the world, would we build great houses for ourselves? No, we would devote ourselves to searching for the truth. Thus the effort we expend building great houses shows that we care more for other people's esteem than we do for the truth.

– 211

A person may ask: 'What shall I do? I can make no sense of the world around me. Should I believe that I count for nothing? Or should I believe that I am God?'

— 227

A dialogue may occur:

'Do you not claim that the beauty and order of nature prove that God exists?'

'No, I do not claim that.'

'Surely your religion makes that claim?'

'No, it does not. Although it is true that God has revealed himself to some people through nature, this is not true for the majority.'

— 244

There is nothing so consistent with reason than the recognition that reason by itself cannot comprehend truth.

— 272

The power of kings is based partly on their strength, and partly on the weakness of those they rule – but mainly on weakness. Indeed, all that is great and important in our lives is based on our weakness. Human weakness is an extremely firm foundation, because nothing is more certain than that people will be weak. Anything based on human strength has an extremely uncertain foundation.

– 330

Tyranny is the desire for one's own gift to dominate all others. People generally excel in only one thing, such as strength, beauty, knowledge or piety. Tyrants claim that the thing in which they excel is more important than the things in which other people excel. But if they understand the gifts of others, they would realise that such dominance is impossible.... Tyranny is also the desire to have by one means what can only be had by another. We should respond differently to different kinds of merit: we should admire beauty, fear strength, believe in knowledge, and respect piety. But the tyrant says: 'I am handsome, so you must fear me.' Or, 'I am strong, so you must admire me.'

– 332

Ordinary people show special honour to those who are highly born. Half-clever people despise them, saying that birth is a matter of chance, not personal merit. Wise people honour them as they wish to be honoured – as they honour all.

– 337

Human beings do not naturally always go in one direction; they sometimes go down, and sometimes up.

– 354

It is surely amazing that people are not amazed at their own weakness. They pursue their various careers with great seriousness, as if they know what they are supposed to be doing. They are convinced of the value of their own skills and abilities. And even when they are beset by failure, they do not conclude that their ambitions are too high; on the contrary, they re-double their efforts. There is no trace of scepticism about themselves; they do not doubt the high opinion they have of their abilities, and they continue to regard themselves as wise. For this reason we need sceptics. Indeed, the case for scepticism is that most people are not sceptics. If all were sceptics, all would be wrong.

– 374

Human weakness is more obvious in those who do not realise they are weak, than in those who do.

— 376

Religious sects derive more strength from their enemies than from their friends.

— 376

Those who talk about their humility are generally proud; and those who regret their pride are usually humble. Those who appear most sceptical often have the most secure grasp; and those who appear most certain in their beliefs, are often very confused.

— 377

It is not good to be too free. It is not good to have all you need.

— 379

Thinking too little about things makes us obstinate; thinking too much about things makes us fanatical.

— 381

When everything is moving at once, nothing seems to be moving — as on board ship. When everyone is moving towards wickedness, no one seems to be moving. But if someone stops, he or she shows up those who are rushing onwards.

— 382

Those who lead disorderly lives tell those who are normal that they are deviating from nature, and they imagine that they themselves are following nature – just as those on board ship leaving port think that the people on shore are moving away. But morality is the same everywhere; and thus objective morality is the fixed point by which all human behaviour should be judged.

– 383

Many things that are certain are contradicted. Many things that are false pass without contradiction. Contradiction is no more an indication of falsehood, than lack of it is an indication of truth.

– 384

It is dangerous to explain to people how similar they are to animals, without pointing out their differences. It is also dangerous to explain to people how different they are from animals, without pointing out their similarities. It is even more dangerous to leave people in ignorance of both, because through comparing themselves with animals they can better understand themselves.

– 418

If other people exalt themselves, I want to humble them. If other people humble themselves, I want to exalt them. How perverse I am to want to contradict other people's opinions of themselves.

— 420

All those contradictions, which seem to take me furthest from religious faith, actually lead me towards religious faith.

— 424

Human beings do not know their place and purpose. They have fallen from their true place, and lost their true purpose. They search everywhere for their place and purpose, with great anxiety. But they cannot find them because they are surrounded by darkness.

— 427

There is enough light for those who desire to see light; and enough darkness for those who prefer darkness.

— 430

People may devote themselves to accumulating wealth, but they should never claim to possess the wealth they acquire. This is because they lack the strength to make it secure. The same is true of knowledge: we may acquire knowledge, but we can never possess it. Illness can remove what we know at any time.

– 436

We desire the truth, but find within ourselves nothing but uncertainty. We seek happiness, but find mainly misery. We are incapable of suppressing the desire for truth and happiness, and yet are incapable of knowing truth and happiness. These frustrated desires remind us how far we have fallen from our true state.

– 437

Our instincts make us feel that our happiness is to be sought outside ourselves. Our desires and emotions push us to look outwards, even when there is nothing to excite us. External objects tempt and entice us, even when we are not thinking about them. Wise men may tell us: withdraw into yourselves, and look within your own souls for happiness. We do not believe them.

– 464

Someone told me the other day that, when he had confessed his sins to a priest, he felt full of joy and hope. Another person told me that, after confessing his sins, he still felt full of remorse and fear. My reaction was that one good man could be made by combining these two, for they each lacked something which the other possessed. This is often the way with different attitudes.

– 530

2

RESOLUTIONS

———◆———

Since our capacity for knowledge is limited, we cannot know everything there is to be known about everything. It is better to know something about everything, rather than everything about something.

– 37

Contemplate the whole of nature in its dazzling beauty and complexity. Contemplate the universe in its awesome vastness; with the earth as a mere speck within it. Then realise that your rational mind cannot comprehend the complexity of nature or the vastness of the universe. Yet where reason must stop, imagination can proceed. The imagination can rejoice in its own simplicity, as compared with nature's complexity; and it can thus find peace by resting in nature's ample bosom. The imagination can rejoice in its own smallness, recognising that within the infinity of space everywhere is the centre.

– 72

If we look honestly at ourselves, we recognise the severe limitations of our knowledge. We cannot possibly comprehend the whole of God's creation. Yet we aspire to comprehend those parts to which our mental capacity bears some proportion. Then we begin to realise that every part of God's creation is connected and linked together; so that by understanding what we can, we have an inkling of the whole.

– 72

Let us see how people define the greatest good, and find out the extent to which their definitions agree. Some say the greatest good consists in virtue; others in obedience to the laws of nature; others in truth; others in total ignorance; others in indolence and self-indulgence; others in abstinence from superficial pleasures; others in serenity and in never being surprised; others in doubt and scepticism. And there are some very wise people who say that the greatest good can never be defined, however strongly we want to define it. That is the finest answer – the agreement to which our disagreements point.

– 73

Imagination is the dominant faculty in human beings. It sometimes leads the mind towards truth, and sometimes towards falsehood. And since there is no means of telling the direction in which it is leading, it is a most unreliable and deceptive master. Not only fools, but wise people also, are led by imagination. And even when reason objects, imagination usually proves too strong. Indeed, imagination in its arrogance treats reason as its enemy; and it takes pleasure in demonstrating its power over reason. Imagination can make people sad or happy, sick or well, rich or poor. It can make people believe or doubt. It can deaden the senses or arouse them. It can raise people's understanding, or it can plunge them into ignorance. It can give far greater pleasure and satisfaction than reason, entertaining the mind with wonderful pictures and sounds. Those who have lively imaginations regard themselves as far superior to those who possess rational intelligence. They are bold and confident in conversation, whereas rational people are cautious and hesitant; thus they win the trust and admiration of their listeners.

— 82

By some quirk of feeling, I dislike people who crack and puff while they are eating. These quirks of feeling carry a great deal of influence in our lives. Should we regard them as natural, and therefore indulge them? No, we should recognise that they cause harm, and resist them.

– 86

When we are well, we wonder how we would manage if we were ill. When we are ill, we take our medicines gratefully; and we manage. We no longer have the emotions, and the desires for entertainment and for social activities, which go with good health; illness extinguishes them. Thus nature adjusts our emotions and desires to our present conditions. The fears we have about illness, when we are well, are therefore irrational.

– 109

From their earliest years children are told to strive for the respect of others, to look after their property, and to win friends – and they are even told to look after their friends' property and reputation. They are burdened with duties to perform, lessons to learn, and exercises to do. They are persuaded that they can never be happy unless their health, their reputation and their wealth are intact; and that if something goes wrong with one of these three, their happiness will be ruined. Thus they feel harassed from the moment they wake up each day. Surely this is a strange way to make people happy? Can we not devise some better method? Let us take away their cares and worries, and allow them to work out for themselves who they are, and what they want to become.

– 143

The saints claim that happiness does not require the stimulus of worldly pleasure. 'But,' answer the sceptics, 'people find great delight in worldly pleasure.' 'That is true,' the saints respond; 'yet pleasure which comes from outside the individual can easily be disturbed or withdrawn, causing great distress.'

– 170

The way of God, who is gentle in all things, is to instil religion into our minds through reasoned arguments, and into our hearts with grace. But if we attempt to instil it into people's minds by force, with threats of retribution, we instil only terror. Indeed much of what passes for religion is terror.

– 185

Many people hate religion. And hatred is deepened because they are afraid it might be true. The cure for this is first to show that religion is not contrary to reason, and thus should be taken seriously. Secondly, make religion attractive, so that good people want it to be true. Thirdly, explain to them that religion can help them to understand themselves, and in this way bring them many blessings.

– 187

The most important choice you have to make is whether or not you seek the truth. If you die without having gained some inkling of the truth, your life will have been wasted. 'But,' you say, 'if truth had wanted me to seek him, he would have left some signs.' He has left signs, but you pay no heed to them. Look for those signs; the reward will be great.

– 236

I would be much more afraid of rejecting religious faith, and later finding out it were true, than of embracing religious faith, and later finding out it were false.

– 241

There are three ways of having faith: reason, habit and inspiration. Christianity will not accept people as its true children unless they have inspiration. This does not mean that Christianity excludes reason and habit. Indeed it requires that we open our minds to the rational foundations of its teachings, and allow our habits of thought and behaviour to be changed. But this change can only be achieved if God inspires it.

– 245

Piety is different from superstition. To carry piety to the point of superstition is to destroy it. Heretics rightly reproach many Christians for their superstitious submission to the Christian dogmas.

– 255

There are very few true and faithful Christians. There are many who believe the Christian creeds; but their belief is founded on superstition, not personal conviction. There are many who do not believe, because they want to be free of any dogmas that may constrain their pursuit of pleasure. There are a few in between. The true Christians are those who believe with both head and heart, and who lead devout lives.

– 256

Faith tells us what the senses cannot; but true faith does not contradict the senses. Faith is above, not against, the senses.

– 265

If we make reason the only judge of truth, our religion will become devoid of mystery. But if we ignore reason, our religion will become absurd and ridiculous. – 273

Do not be astonished to see simple people believing in religion without argument. God makes them love him and recognise their own need for him. He inclines their hearts to believe in him. We can never believe – we can never possess a real and effective faith – unless God inclines our hearts.

– 284

Instead of complaining that God has hidden himself, we would do better to thank him for revealing himself as much as he has – and to thank him for not revealing himself to clever people who are full of pride, and therefore unworthy of knowing him.

Two sorts of people know God. There are those who are humble of heart, and are content with their lowly state; these people may be highly intelligent or quite simple. And there are those who would prefer that God did not exist, but are perceptive enough to see the truth.

– 288

True wisdom makes us like children.

– 291

It is right to follow those who are right; it is prudent to follow those who are mighty. Right without might is helpless; might without right is tyrannical. Right without might is constantly challenged; might without right is constantly denounced…. Right is open to dispute; might is easily recognised, and is beyond dispute. Right cannot be made mighty, because might challenges right, calling it unjust. Therefore we must strive to make the mighty right.

– 298

To respect others means putting yourself out for their sake. This should be done even when it seems pointless. An act of respect is a way of saying: 'I should certainly put myself out if you really needed it, since I am willing to do so even when you do not need it.' Acts of respect also mark out those whom you esteem highly. If respect meant sitting in an armchair, we would be showing respect to everyone; so there would be no way of showing special esteem. We can only show that we value another person by making sacrifices for them.

– 317

Wise people prefer the hunt to the capture.

– 324

Knowledge has two extremes which meet. One is the pure natural ignorance of the infant at birth. The other is reached by great minds which have passed through the entire range of human knowledge, only to find that they know nothing of the truth, and have come back to the same ignorance from which they started. This latter state is a wise ignorance which knows itself. Those who stand between these two extremes have put their natural ignorance behind them, but have not yet attained wise ignorance. They have a smattering of knowledge, and imagine that they understand almost everything. They are profoundly misguided, and can do great damage.

– 327

What part of us feels pleasure? Is it the hands, the arms, the muscles or the blood? No. So it is obviously something immaterial.

– 339

Humanity is only a reed, the weakest reed in nature. But humanity is a thinking reed. The universe does not make any effort to crush humanity; human beings are easily killed. But even if the rest of the universe were to turn against humanity, humanity alone would understand what was happening – because humanity alone possesses the power of thought. All our dignity consists in this power. Our survival depends on this power. Our knowledge of morality, and thence how we should behave, depends on this power. So let us strive to think well.   – 347

I spent much of my life believing that justice is possible. And this belief is correct, for God has chosen to reveal his justice. But I did not realise that God alone determines justice; and in this I was wrong. I put my faith in human standards of justice; and so I thought that I was able to discern what is just. Gradually I recognised that I was making numerous unjust judgments, and so I began to distrust both myself and others. I saw that all societies and all people must continually change, and I decided therefore that standards of justice must also continually change. Finally I accepted that, since I myself am continually changing, I should never claim to understand the nature of justice. And since reaching that conclusion, my opinion has never changed.

– 375

The easiest means of putting your emotions and passions in order is to imagine you have only a week to live.

– 386

Human beings attain greatness through knowing they are wretched; a tree does not know it is wretched.

– 397

People should try to know themselves. This may not help them to find the truth. But it does help them to organise their lives well – and that is the most important task.

– 405

Human beings think and act according to custom. Once people become accustomed to religion, they find it easier to accept it. In the same way, once people become accustomed to a particular man being king, they find it easier to submit to his authority.

– 419

Those who choose to praise the greatness of human knowledge are fools. Those who despise the paucity of human knowledge are fools. And those who choose to ignore human knowledge, and to divert themselves with idle amusements, are also fools. But those who crawl on their knees in search of knowledge are truly wise.

— 421

Let people love themselves, because they have within them great capacity for good; but do not let them love their capacity for evil. Let people hate themselves, because their capacity for good remains unfilled; but do not let them hate this capacity. Thus people should both love and hate themselves.

— 423

All people seek happiness. There are no exceptions. They differ on the means they use, but their goal is the same. Those who go to war and those who do not have an equal desire for happiness, but they interpret it in a different way. Human beings do not take even the smallest step, except in the hope of increasing their happiness. This is the motive of every act of every person, including those who go and hang themselves.

Yet for many years no one without faith has ever reached the goal to which all people are striving. They all complain about their condition – princes and their subjects, nobles and commoners, old and young, strong and weak, educated and ignorant, healthy and sick, in every country, at every time, and of all ages and conditions.

Surely this should convince us that we are incapable of attaining happiness purely by our own efforts. Unfortunately the example of others seems to teach us little. We observe subtle differences between ourselves and others, and conclude that we will not be disappointed as they have been. So, while we are dissatisfied with our present condition, we continue along our accustomed path, going from one misfortune to the next, until death intervenes and stops us.

Yet the craving for happiness is the trace of past happiness; it tells us that once human beings were truly happy. The craving may be compared with an empty space that needs to be filled. We try to fill it with everything we see around us, but it remains empty. It is an infinite abyss that can only be filled by an infinite being – by God himself.

God alone can bring happiness. And since human beings abandoned God, nothing in nature has been found to take his place – stars, sky, earth, elements, plants, vegetables, animals, insects, calves, snakes, fever, plague, war, famine, vice, adultery, incest. People look for happiness in all these things, even when they lead to their own destruction. But they never find it. Some believe they will find happiness if they can exert authority over others; some think they will find it through intellectual inquiry and knowledge; some think they will find it in pleasure. Wise people, however, realise that happiness cannot be found in particular objects.

– 428

To make people happy religion must show to people that a God exists whom we are bound to love; that happiness can only be found through loving him; and that the sole cause of unhappiness is to be cut off from him. Religion must acknowledge the darkness which fills us, hindering us from knowing and loving God; and it must recognise too the desires which can lead us away from him. And it must offer an explanation of these things. Most importantly, religion must hold a cure for our condition, and show us how to obtain this cure. These are the criteria by which we should judge the religions of the world.

– 430

When we think of our own wretchedness, we are amazed that God should wish us to unite with him. Yet some people imagine that God's mercy is incapable of reaching us, because our wretchedness puts us so far below him. By what right do they express this view? In recognising our wretchedness, we should recognise that we are incapable of measuring God's mercy – that we have no rights to impose limits on it. Certainly we should be disturbed at our spiritual and moral state; but for that reason we should never dare to question God's mercy. God invites us to love and know him; and if we accept his invitation, he will make us capable of loving and knowing him.

– 430

If human beings were not made for God, why are they only happy in union with God? If human beings were made for God, why are they often opposed to God?

– 438

Humanity's true nature, humanity's true virtue, and humanity's true religion are so closely connected that they cannot be known separately.

– 442

How can you learn to love yourself? Imagine that each part of your body – each limb and organ – was conscious. Since all the parts are dependent on one another, they would all love one another. Thus your whole body would be filled with love for itself.

– 474

When we sit or kneel down to think about God, our minds are easily distracted, and we find ourselves thinking about something else. This reminds us how feeble we are in spirit.

– 478

It is quite certain that there is no goodness without knowledge of God; that the closer one comes to that knowledge, the happier one is; and that ultimate happiness is to know God fully. It is equally certain that the further one goes away from knowledge of God, the more unhappy one becomes; and that ultimate unhappiness is to have no inkling of God.

– 499

Why has God instituted prayer? First, to enter a direct relationship with human beings. Second, to draw us to him as the source of all virtue. Third, to strengthen our efforts in becoming virtuous.

– 513

Be comforted. It is not from yourself that you should expect to discover the truth. On the contrary, you should expect to discover the truth by expecting nothing from yourself.

– 517

Knowing God without knowing our own wretchedness engenders pride. Knowing our own wretchedness without knowing God engenders despair.

– 527

How little pride true Christians feel when they believe themselves united with God! How little they grovel when they liken themselves to earthworms! It is a fine attitude of mind with which to meet life and death, good and evil.

– 538

Good behaviour may make you lovable, but it will not make you happy. Only religion can make you both lovable and happy.

– 542

God makes the soul aware that he is its sole good; that in him alone it can find peace; and that only through loving him it will experience joy. At the same time God makes the soul loathe obstacles which hold it back and hinder it from loving God with all its strength. Through God the soul hates its own selfishness.... And God also assures the soul that he can cure this selfishness.

– 544

I love all people as my brothers and sisters, because Christ loves and redeems them. I love poverty because he loved it. I love wealth because it gives me the means of helping the poor. I keep faith with everyone. I do not return evil to those who have done evil to me, but wish that they and me alike should receive neither good nor evil at the hands of others. I try to be fair, genuine, sincere and loyal to all people; and I feel special affection towards those whom God has joined intimately to me. I know that whether I am alone or in the company of others, I am in the sight of God.

– 550

The world exists for the exercise of mercy and judgment. People seem as if they were created not to be God's friends, but to be his enemies. Yet by his grace he grants them enough light to enable them to find him. Thus they may choose to become his friends, or to remain his enemies.

– 584

To be religious is both infinitely wise and infinitely foolish.

– 588

I look at the blind and wretched state of humanity. I see that, left to themselves, human beings exist in a dark cloud of ignorance. They are lost in a remote corner of the universe, not knowing who put them there, or what their purpose is, or what will happen to them when they die. Humanity's ignorance moves me to terror. I feel like a man who has been transported in his sleep to some terrifying desert island, and who then wakes up feeling utterly lost and unable to find any means of escape. But then I marvel that this wretched state does not move people to despair. I ask the people around me, who in every way are similar to me, whether they are better informed than I am; and they say that they are not. They seek and find some external objects to which they become attached and addicted. But I have never been able to form such attachments. And since it is likely that there is a dimension of reality apart from what I can see, I devote myself to discovering this dimension.

– 693

Truth is so rare and lies are so common that, unless we love the truth, we shall never recognise it.

– 864

3
THE WAGER

We know that the infinite exists without knowing its nature, just as we know that numbers are not finite. Thus there is an infinite number, even though we do not know what it is. This infinite number is neither even nor odd, because it cannot be changed by adding a unit. And yet it is a number, and every number is even or odd.

Therefore we may say that God exists, even though we do not know what he is.... We do not know the size of God, nor the time since his inception because he is infinite and eternal. Yet by faith we know his existence, and ultimately we shall encounter him....

Who, then, can blame Christians for not being able to give rational grounds for their beliefs? They do not profess a rational foundation for their faith. They declare openly that faith is folly; so no one should complain that they cannot prove it. If they could prove it, their declaration of folly would be dishonest. The lack of proof shows that they do not lack honesty.

'Yes,' you agree, 'but although this absolves them

from charges of dishonesty, it does not absolve them from charges of irrationality.' We can respond to your point by saying, 'Either God exists, or he does not exist.' To which view should we be inclined? Reason cannot decide this question. An infinite distance separates us from the answer. At the far end of this distance a coin is being spun which will come heads or tails. How will you wager? Reason cannot prove your choice right or wrong.

Do not condemn as wrong those who have made a choice, since your choice is not better than theirs. 'No,' you reply, 'I will not condemn them for making a particular choice. But I condemn them for making any choice. The one who calls heads and the one who calls tails are equally at fault. The proper response is not to wager at all.'

Yes, but you must wager. On that there is no choice; you are already committed. Which will you choose? Since a choice must be made, we must see which is the least bad. You have two things to lose: truth and happiness. You have two things at stake: your reason and your happiness. And you have two things to avoid: error and misery. Since you must necessarily choose, your reason is no more affronted by choosing one rather than the other. So this point is cleared up. How about your happiness? Let us weigh up the gain and the loss in calling heads that God exists. If you win, you win everything. If you lose, you lose nothing. So do not hesitate; wager that God exists....

Let us change the odds, and assume that there is one chance of winning against a large number of chances of losing. Yet that number is finite. The prize of winning, by contrast is infinite: it is infinite and eternal happiness. This still leaves no choice: where the prize is infinite, but the chances of losing are finite, you must place everything on winning the prize....

'This is unfair,' you protest. 'I am not free to act and speak as I want. I am being forced to wager. I am not free, but am in chains. My nature is such that I cannot believe. So what do you want me to do?'

'Your protests are justified,' we reply. 'But you should understand that your own selfish desires are the obstacles preventing belief. Thus, although reason impels you towards faith, your desires impede you. The solution, then, lies not in further argument, in which you multiply the proofs of God's existence; but rather in controlling your desires. You want to find faith, and yet you do not know the road. You want to be cured of unbelief, and you ask for a remedy. Learn from those who were once like you, and now wager all they have. They are people who know the road you wish to follow, and you have been cured of the affliction from which you suffer. Follow their path. They began to believe as if they believed, participating in religious worship, and obeying the moral teachings of religion; and gradually their souls followed their behaviour – they became quite docile.'

'That is what I am afraid of,' you reply.

'But you have no reason for fear,' we say, 'because you have nothing to lose. What harm can come to you from choosing this course? You will become faithful, honest, humble, grateful and charitable; you will become a true and sincere friend. Certainly you will no longer enjoy the pleasures that destroy the soul and weaken the body; but you will be far happier. You will benefit even in this life. And at every step you take, you will become more certain of the future benefits. In the end you will realise that you have wagered on something without either risk or cost.

– 233

4
AGAINST INDIFFERENCE

———◆———

Let those who attack religion first see what religion is. If religion boasted that it could see God clearly, or that there was plain and manifest evidence of his existence, then the opponents of religion could rightly say that these claims were dishonest. But in fact religion acknowledges that God has hidden himself, and that human beings are lost in a dark cloud of ignorance. Thus it tries to establish two facts: firstly that God has left signs of himself, which can be recognised by those who genuinely seek him; and secondly he has disguised these signs in such a way that those who do not seek him will not perceive them. So it is absurd for those who oppose religion to protest that they cannot see evidence of God's existence; they cannot see it, because they are not genuinely seeking it.

If their opposition were to be effective, they would have to make every effort to seek this evidence everywhere, even to the extent of accepting instruction from religious teachers – and at the end of this diligent search, still claim that God has left no signs of himself. They would then be true opponents of religion. But to my knowledge no one has ever acted in this way....

I reply to those opponents that their ignorance about religion is utterly foolish and irrational. They treat religion as if it were a trivial matter, of only shallow interest. Yet the questions it raises are vitally important, affecting us so deeply that any sensitive person should want to grapple with them. The choice of whether to believe or reject the tenets of religion determines the course of our lives, influencing every decision we make and action we take.

So our chief interest and duty should be to enlighten ourselves on matters of religion. And that is why, among unbelievers, I make an absolute distinction between those who strive with all their might to learn about religion, and those who do not bother to think seriously about it. I feel great compassion towards those who sincerely regret their doubt, regarding it as a grave misfortune, and who make every effort to resolve it, searching for truth with the utmost seriousness....

But those who are negligent and indifferent towards matters of religion fill me with irritation rather than pity. Their attitude astounds and appals me; it seems utterly monstrous. My feelings are not prompted by pious zeal, but by concern for their lack of self-esteem, and for their blindness to their own interests. They seem to suffer from wilful stupidity.

One needs no great spiritual discernment to realise that there is no true and permanent happiness in this world, that our pleasures are transient, that our afflictions are unending, and that death – which threatens us at every moment – will within a few years certainly overcome us. And at death we face the dreadful alternative of total annihilation or eternal misery.

Nothing could be more real or more terrifying than that. We can try to put a brave face on it; but even the most illustrious person on earth confronts this prospect. Let us think about this, and then conclude that the only good thing in life is the possibility of a life above and beyond it. Indeed it is only by recognising this higher and greater level of existence, and by coming nearer to it, that we have any inkling of the happiness for which we yearn.

– 194

5
THE MEMORIAL

———————————

The year of grace 1654

Monday 23 November, feast of Saint Clement, pope and martyr, and of others in the martyrology.

Eve of Saint Chrysogonus, martyr and others.

From about half-past ten in the evening until half-past midnight.

Fire

God of Abraham, God of Isaac, God of Jacob, not of philosophers and scholars.

Certainty, certainty, heartfelt joy, peace.

God of Jesus Christ.

God of Jesus Christ.

My God and your God.

Your God shall be my God.

The world forgotten, and everything except God.

He can only be found by the ways taught in the Gospels.

Greatness of the human soul.

Righteous Father, the world has not known you, but I know you.

Joy, joy, joy, tears of joy.

I had cut myself off from him.

Just as others have forsaken him the fount of living water.

My God, will you forsake me?

Let me not be cut off from him ever again.

This is life eternal, that we might know you, the only true God, and know Jesus Christ whom you sent.

Jesus Christ.

Jesus Christ.

6

THE STAGES OF CONVERSION

When God decides to enter an intimate relationship with a soul, his first action is to bestow profound knowledge and insight. This enables the soul to reflect upon herself and her circumstances in a manner that is entirely new.

This enlightenment disturbs the soul, instilling within her great guilt at the foolish pleasures in which she used to indulge. The soul now finds that these pleasures hold no attraction. Indeed, although the soul once enjoyed them with great freedom and ease of heart, the very thought of them has become repulsive.

Yet the holy joy which God offers is invisible, so it cannot excite the soul in the way that visible, earthly pleasures once did. Worse still, to the newly converted soul the joy of God seems bleak and austere, demanding great effort for little reward. Thus the soul feels extremely confused and depressed: earthly pleasures have lost their appeal, but heavenly pleasures appear to be no substitute.

Despite this confusion, the soul cannot return to her former state. She sees clearly that all she earlier loved is transient and will eventually perish, and this fills her with horror. With every moment that passes she is being drawn further from her earthly attachments; she feels them slipping from her grasp, and she knows that a day will dawn when she is stripped of them completely. She now knows clearly that these attachments were brittle and empty; and at death they would suddenly have disappeared, leaving her alone and defenceless. Indeed, she feels astonished that she had not realised her folly sooner, and thus had more time to acquire solid and permanent treasure, which would sustain her both in this life and in the life to come.

Thus the soul comes to despise as worthless all that is destined to perish: mind and body; human relationships; possessions and reputation; authority and knowledge; health, and even life itself. The soul, recognising that she herself is immortal, finds that anything less than immortal is powerless to satisfy her. She seeks permanence and stability.

The soul begins to feel astonished that she could have been so deluded in the past. She reflects on the length of time she has been blind to her true condition; and she reflects too on the number of souls that remain deluded. She cannot understand how she failed to see such an obvious truth: that an immortal soul can never be satisfied by things that are mortal and perishable. Her confusion thus deepens – a state which does her a great deal of good. On top of her confusion come anxiety and anger. She is appalled at the vast number of deluded souls that are destined to face death without protection. And she is furious that this number seems to lend authority to their delusion.

Confusion, anxiety and anger gradually give way to a calmer and more reflective state. She looks back on the transient things to which she once aspired, and to which most people continue to aspire: wealth, fame and knowledge. And she realises that they are not in themselves evil or sinful. Indeed they can serve good purposes, and yield lawful and righteous satisfaction; and she herself derived a measure of genuine satisfaction from them. The evil lies in making them the primary and sole sources of satisfaction.

The soul now develops a strange and paradoxical attitude. On the one hand she feels deeply humble, recognising her utter dependence on God. On the other hand she feels herself to be above the common run of people. She condemns their behaviour, despises their values, holds their worldly wisdom in contempt, and weeps over their blindness. But eventually she decides that, instead of despising other people, she should love them. And she realises that love is the most durable and stable of all spiritual qualities. Thus she devotes all her efforts to the acquisition of love – knowing that even if the objects of love eventually change or disappear, love itself can never be taken away.

Love for other people necessarily lifts the soul upwards to the source of love. The soul now desires with great intensity to find and reach that source. She knows that the source is not within her; nor is it in any of the things of this earth. The source of love, she reckons, is the supreme object of desire, a shadowless light that can never change or disappear.

The eyes of the soul look higher and higher. They do not stop at heaven, nor the angels, nor even the most perfect created beings. They pass every creature, until they see the throne of God himself. The soul knows at once that here is true, complete and eternal happiness; and that this happiness, once experienced, can never fade.

The soul knows that she has not yet reached a condition in which she can receive this happiness. She is still lacking in virtue. But now she sees how she can grow in virtue: she must learn to see the creator in every creature, and thence to love the creator in every creature. Only God is truly worthy of love; so true love of other creatures is only possible through loving God within them. Despite acknowledging her own lack of virtue, the soul rejoices at seeing the path towards virtue.

With these new thoughts the soul begins to contemplate the elevated ways of her creator. She is aware that in comparison with God she is worthless; but, far from resenting her humble status, she rejoices in it. Nonetheless she feels frustrated because she cannot express herself adequately to God. No words are sufficient to describe her feelings of awe and wonder at his glorious beauty, nor her overwhelming desire to be utterly absorbed by him. She tries to praise him in words, but eventually becomes exhausted by her efforts; so instead she worships him in silence. She knows that he does not benefit from her worship yet equally she knows that he has created her in order to worship him.

In her silence she is suddenly overwhelmed with astonishment at his mercy – that in his infinite majesty he has been willing to reveal himself to a mere worm like herself. She makes a firm resolution always to be thankful. And she is even more perplexed that she ever preferred earthly things to the joy which God gives. This remembrance of her earlier life makes her astonishment grow ever greater: her sinful stupidity should have incurred God's wrath, and yet, far from punishing her, he has saved her.

She earnestly prays that, as God has been pleased to reveal himself to her, he will now become her guide, planting within her the wisdom that will eventually lead her into his presence. Since God is the sole object of her desire, she wants to come to him only by the path and at the speed which he decrees. He himself shall be her way, her companion, and her destination.

She now acts like a traveller who wonders which road to follow: she consults others who are better informed about the path to God. She seeks out people who have walked along that path for many years, and are familiar with it, believing that through their advice God will guide her.

She is now firmly committed to spending the rest of her life in conformity to his will. She is conscious that she remains weak, and hence is liable to fall back into old sinful habits; and she knows that by her own strength she would not be able to pull herself upright again. Thus she pleads with God to provide the strength which she lacks.

By this means the soul recognises that she has a duty to worship God, since she is his creation; that she should constantly offer him thanks and praise; that she should follow his path of virtue; and that she is entirely dependent on his grace.

7
FOR THE GOOD USE OF SICKNESS

Lord, you are gentle in all your ways; and your mercy is such that not only the blessings, but also the misfortunes, of your people are the fruits of your compassion. Grant that I may not respond to my present condition as if I had no faith. Grant that as a Christian I may still acknowledge you as my Father, regardless of my condition, since changes in my physical state signify no changes in yours. You are no less divine when you bring suffering, than when you confer favours.

You gave me health that I might serve you; yet I merely abused this gift. Now, therefore, you send me ill-health in order to correct me. Do not let me abuse this correction by showing impatience. When I was healthy, I failed to serve you well, and so with justice you have taken away my health; let me now serve you well in illness. The sickness of my soul is such that even your favours do me harm; let this physical illness which you send bring healing to my soul. My heart, which was strong, was filled with love for the pleasures of this world; destroy that strength in order to make me holy. Use the weakness of my body to render me incapable of worldly pleasure, so that at last I may find joy in you alone.

O God, before whom I must render an exact account of all my actions at the end of my life and at the end of time; who wants all people on earth to obey your will; who seeks to soften the hearts of sinners while they remain on earth; who at the moment of death separates our souls from our bodies and from all the pleasures our bodies have loved; who will snatch away from me all the things to which I have attached myself, and on which I have set my heart.... I praise you, O God, and I bless you. Every day I give thanks that you have brought me down, putting me in a condition where I can no longer enjoy the mild and easy pleasures of good health, and where the pleasures of this world have lost their taste. For my own spiritual health you have in large measure destroyed the health of my body. You deny me false joys now, in order to bestow upon me true joys later.

Grant that in this condition of physical sickness I may consider myself dead to the world, stripped of all those things to which I am attached, alone in your presence, imploring you in your mercy to turn my heart towards you. In this state give me the greatest of all consolations: the knowledge that this death in life is a prelude to life in death, for which you judge me worthy. Since you have intervened in this way prior to my death, give me the humility to atone for the sins I have committed during my life. In this way I shall find mercy in your presence.

Grant, O God, that I may accept with silent praise the way in which you have ordered my life, including your decision to send me this sickness. When my body was free of pain, my soul was bitter with sin; now that my body is full of pain, let my soul taste the sweetness of your grace.

Yet I recognise and acknowledge, O God, that my heart is very stubborn, and that it is gripped by vain ideas and opinions, and by cares, anxieties and attachments. As a result neither sickness nor health, nor the wise counsel of my priests, nor the reading of spiritual books, nor even the Bible itself, nor acts of charity and penance, nor miracles, nor the sacraments, nor the Holy Communion, nor any effort of mine, nor the efforts of the entire world, could have even begun the work of my conversion. Without you all these things are worthless; only when they are founded on your grace do they possess spiritual value.

So I cry to you, almighty God, begging from you the gift that all of nature cannot bestow. I would not be so bold as to ask your help, if I could obtain this gift elsewhere. But this conversion of the heart, which I desperately seek, is beyond the capacity of nature and the master of my heart. To whom shall I cry, Lord, to whom shall I go for help, if not to you?

Nothing that is less than God himself can satisfy me. It is God himself whom I require and seek. To you, God and to you alone I turn. Open my heart, Lord and come into this place of rebellion, this place which is occupied by evil vices, and be like a conquering army. Your enemies within my heart are strong; but in your strength you can defeat and bind them, taking from them the treasure which they had seized. Take for yourself, Lord, my affection, which the enemies had stolen; it belongs to you, and has your image stamped upon it....

How happy is the heart, my God, that can love an object so beautiful as you, an object that will never do it the least dishonour. How happy is the heart that can rest in an object as wholesome as you. I well know that I cannot devote myself to worldly pleasures without displeasing you, and without causing harm and dishonour to myself; yet in truth the world is still the main object of my delight. How happy, O God, is the soul whose delight is in you, and is able to devote herself wholly to loving you without any scruple or reserve. How secure and durable is her happiness; her faith and confidence will never be betrayed. For you, O Lord, endure forever; neither life nor death can separate the soul that loves you from the object of her love....

Bring to perfection, O my God, the good inclinations which you have put within me. Let goodness be my goal, my inspiration, and my motive. Use the abilities which you have given me for your purposes. I know that my prayers have so little merit that you are not compelled to answer them. Yet I also know that you have fashioned my soul so that she may be utterly devoted to you. Therefore I feel able to look to you for mercy, trusting that in your mercy you will turn my soul to you. All the natural impulses of my heart can only offend you, unless you incline them to your love. I thank you that you are now doing this....

Uproot in me, O Lord, all self-pity, all tendency to dwell on my own sufferings. Uproot in me all longing for the things of this earth, for the worldly pleasures which can never satisfy the soul. Uproot in me anything that is not directed to your glory. Clothe me in sorrow, the sorrow that my sins have caused you. May my sufferings bring me closer to you; may they be a channel of grace and a means of my conversion.

Henceforth let me ask neither health nor life itself, except in order to devote both to your service. Let me exist for you, with you, and in you.

FURTHER READING

There are numerous translations of *Pensées*. Apart from differences in the style of the translator, they vary in the way they order Pascal's thoughts. Some use the original ordering, while others attempt to put them in themes chosen by the translator. Both the Penguin Classics and the Everyman series published by J. M. Dent include translations of *Pensées* and the *Provincial Letters*.

PHILOSOPHERS OF THE SPIRIT

Also in this series

Hildegard

A twelfth-century German mystic, Hildegard is being rediscovered today both as a musical composer and as a spiritual prophet of the environmental movement. In her visions she saw the Logos – the Word of God – in all living things. And she saw that human beings can Wnd inner peace and tranquillity only if they recognise their spiritual unity with all animals and plants.

As this new collection of her writings reveals, her insights into the human psyche and its relationship with the whole created order seem astonishingly modern.

PHILOSOPHERS OF THE SPIRIT

Also in this series

Kierkegaard

- Is truth objective?
- Can we make real moral choices, or are our choices pre-determined?
- Who are the true saints and heroes of this world?

Kierkegaard, the nineteenth-century Danish philosopher, is both one of the most difficult and one of the most attractive thinkers of the modern period. He is regarded as the founder of existentialism.

This selection of his works, together with an easily readable summary of the principles of his thought and an outline of his life, offers a straightforward introduction to his complex ideas.

PHILOSOPHERS OF THE SPIRIT